THE
BEACON

A Collection of Poems

THE
BEACON

A Collection of Poems

EMERSON CUSTIS

ARPress
ILLUMINATING IDEAS
EMPOWERING VOICES

ARPress

45 Dan Road Suite 5

Canton, MA 02021

Hotline: 1(888) 821-0229

Fax: 1(508) 545-7580

Ordering Information:

Quantity sales. Special discounts are available on quantity purchases by corporations, associations, and others. For details, contact the publisher at the address above.

Printed in the United States of America.

ISBN-13: Softcover 979-8-89356-817-2
eBook 979-8-89356-818-9

Library of Congress Control Number: 2024905289

INTRODUCTION

I have searched the world over for the answers to life's most challenging questions. Amid that search, answers rang out to me in rhyme and verse. I mean that literally, two of these poems appeared to me out of thin air. The rest just flowed from the opening that they made. I give these for the enlightenment of those who find poetry a means to understanding their lives and expanding their horizons. The written or spoken word, are the most powerful forces in the universe. The universe began with it and all that we see today, is only possible with words. Read and feel the power of words.

HARDCORE REALITY

What is reality to me?
The question comes constantly,
Thought deceit can hide the truth,
and cover you like a fog.
Now comes the time you must see,
The hidden truth within that fog.
For you are truth and this to me,
Is all that reality can truly be.
When I communicate with thee,
what you hear is your reality.
And when you see the stars on high,
Then feel to touch you must learn to fly.
Then reality has passed you by.
For life is but a probability,
and all that is, is your reality.
Truth about life is hard to swallow,
So the game of life you gladly follow.
When deep within the truth remains,
Reality is why you came.

CHRISTIAN AWARENESS

Without consciousness, pray tell,
Your life is but an empty shell.
Then fear and ignorance contains,
Your consciousness on ball and chain.

With introspection of the same
Your conscious flame will light again.
Doors will open from within
And show you worlds that do not end.

So close your eyes, and then begin,
To find your answers from within.
You'll find you're spirit to the brim,
And only then will you be born again.

FAITH (SECURITY)

There is nothing to fear,

as long as you are here.

Stop looking at the world you know

For the reality you hold dear.

You've got this funny notion,

from life's hardships and its pains.

But if you look within yourself,

you'll know just why you came.

You are you and I am me,

there's god in between.

So know thyself within thyself,

and god will see you through.

MEETING GOD

You were on your way home when you died.

It was a car accident. Nothing particularly remarkable, but fatal nonetheless. You left behind a wife and two children. It was a painless death. The EMTs tried their best to save you, but to no avail. Your body was so utterly shattered you were better off, trust me.

And that's when you met me. "What... what happened?" You asked. "Where am I?" "You died," I said, matter-of-factly. No point mincing words. "There was a... a truck and it was skidding..." "Yup." I said. "I... I died?" "Yup. But don't feel bad about it. Everyone dies." I said. You looked around. There was nothingness. Just you and me. "What is this place?" You asked. "Is this the afterlife?" "More or less," I said. "Are you god?" You asked. "Yup." I replied. "I'm God." "My kids... my wife," you said. "What about them?" "Will they be alright?" "That's what I like to see," I said. "You just died and your main concern is your family. That's good stuff right there." You looked at me with fascination. To you, I didn't look like God. I just looked like some man. Some vague authority figure. More of a grammar school teacher than the almighty.

"Don't worry," I said. "They'll be fine. Your kids will remember you as perfect in every way. They didn't have time to grow contempt for you. Your wife will cry on the outside, but will be secretly relieved." "To be fair, your marriage was falling apart. If it's any consolation, she'll feel very guilty for feeling relieved."

"Oh," you said. "So what happens now? Do I go to heaven or hell or something?" "Neither," I said. "You'll be reincarnated." "Ah," you said. "So the Hindus were right." "All the religions are right in their own way," I said. "Walk with me." You followed along as we strolled in the void. "Where are we going?" "Nowhere in particular," I said. "It's just nice to walk while we talk." "So what's the point, then?" You asked. "When I get reborn, I'll just be a blank slate, right? A baby. So all my experiences and everything I did in this life won't matter?"

"Not so!" I said. "You have within you all the knowledge and experiences of all your past lives. You just don't remember them right now." I stopped walking and took you by the shoulders. "Your soul is more magnificent, beautiful, and gigantic than you can possibly imagine. A human mind can only contain a tiny fraction of what you are. It's like sticking your finger in a glass of water to see if it's hot or cold. You put a tiny part of yourself into the vessel, and when you bring it back out, you've gained all the experiences it had." "You've been a human for the last 34 years, so you haven't stretched out yet and felt the rest of your immense consciousness. If we hung out here for longer, you'd start remembering everything. But there's no point doing that between each life." "How many times have I been reincarnated then?" "Oh, lots. Lots and lots. And into lots of different lives." I said. "This time around you'll be a Chinese peasant girl in 540 A.D." "Wait, what?" You stammered. "You're sending me back in time?" "Well, I guess technically. Time, as you know it, only exists in your universe. Things are different where I come from." "Where you come from?" You pondered. "Oh, sure!" I explained. "I come from somewhere. Somewhere else. And there's others like me. I know you'll want to know what it's like there but you honestly won't understand."

"Oh." You said, a little let down. "But wait, if I get reincarnated to other places in time, could I have interacted with myself at some point?" "Sure. Happens all the time. And with both lives only aware of their own timespan, you don't even know its happening." "So what's the point of it all?" "Seriously?" I asked. "Seriously? You're asking me for the meaning of life? Isn't that a little stereotypical?" "Well, it's a reasonable question." You persisted. I looked in your eye. "The meaning of life, the reason I made this whole universe, is for you to mature." "You mean mankind? You want us to mature?" "No. Just you. I made this whole universe for you. With each new life you grow and mature, and become a larger and greater intellect." "Just me? What about everyone else?" "There is no one else," I said. "In this universe, there's just you, and me." You stared blankly at me. "But all the people on Earth..." "All you. Different incarnations of you." "Wait. I'm everyone!?" "Now you're getting it." I said, with a congratulatory slap on the back. "I'm every human who ever lived?" "Or who will ever live, yes." "I'm Abraham Lincoln?" "And you're John Wilkes Booth." I added. "I'm Hitler?" You said, appalled. "And you're the millions he killed." "I'm Jesus?" "And you're everyone who followed him." You fell silent.

"Every time you victimized someone," I said, "You were victimizing yourself. Every act of kindness you've done, you've done to yourself. Every happy and sad moment ever experienced by any human was, or will be, experienced by you." "Why?" You asked me. "Why do all this?" "Because someday, you will become like me. Because that's what you are. You're one of my kind. You're my child." "Whoa." You said, incredulous. "You mean I'm a god?" "No. Not yet. You're a fetus You're still growing. Once you've lived every human life throughout all time, you will have grown enough to be born." "So the whole universe," you said. "It's just..." "An egg of sorts." I answered. "Now it's time for you to move on to your next life." And I sent you on your way.

By Anonymous. Transcribed by Mac Davis for Philosophy Circle's reading catalog *:-< sigh

UNDERSTANDING

For understanding we search to see,
A sign that life gave us the key,
To rightly know that you and me,
Are interacting as we need to be.

See God in creation had a plan,
That good intent was a part of every man,
And if through those eyes everyone you see,
Then understanding has become a part of thee.

You see through eyes focused by belief,
Then understanding is your only relief,
You see, the key to each and every event,
Is the love that was the original intent.

ADAMANT

Adamant, adamant,
Or so it would seem,
Adamant is innocent,
And God knows what it means.
The truth we say is adamant,
Is somewhere in-between.
For adamant may not present
The truth on which you lean.
So next when you are adamant,
Be sure to get the facts.
Do not something you might regret,
When the truth comes rolling back.

AS YOU BELIEVE

Dawn breaks in the morning sky,
Evening waits as the day goes by.
Lightning strikes in the mist of a storm,
While man waits for Gabriel's horn.

God in creation shows man His face,
While man competes in his religious race.
The Holy Spirit he calls for direction,
When all that is, is the man-God connection.

God's power, the radio squawks is real.
Know thyself and that power you'll feel.
He willed that man should live and grow.
And, as you believe, so shall you know.

Man's lack of knowledge is why he fell,
Because he believes, he'll go to hell.
Yes, as you believe, so shall it be unto you,
Believe in truth, and it'll see you through.

BORN AGAIN

Look inside and find the key,

to the door of answers inside of thee.

Look to the east and get your Strength .

And there find your will, heritage sent.

Mind and matter are one in the same.

Mind over matter is your name.

Open your mind to telepathy,

and with those eyes you will truly see.

Fly little man-child and spread your wings,

and take your mind to finer things.

The power to move mountains faith will bring,

return little spirit, to thyself again.

The power of god deep in your soul,

will give the power yet untold.

Grow up little man-child and learn to fly,

I'll see you later, When you kiss the sky.

LOVE ME NOT MY BROTHER

The spirit of human pride,
Is a well of ignorance deep inside.
Black, white, yellow, brown, and red,
Five reasons mankind can't get ahead.

But listen my brother, listen here.
Look inside and conquer your fear,
Of who is right and who is wrong,
All tell those ignorant thoughts begone.
Love made a man, and gave him a name.
Tho' different colors, He made all the same.
Stand tall, proud spirit, be what you be.

Take not advice from poetry.
Knowledge is love, and ignorance is hate.
Which will you become, I can hardly wait.
Be strong, proud spirit and never see,
The beauty of love, inside of thee.
You see, that which is perceived in one,
Is inside the other.
Yet, you love me not, my brother.

PICTURE MIND

Pretty picture that I see,
I give you life inside of me.
But reality has set you free.
Now I exsist inside of thee.

This, a moment in our life,
has delivered us some inner sight.
Trust will turn on wisdom's light,
'ere we use our common right.

Right to know and understand,
the things that knowing will demand.
I see now picture why you stand,
to tease the mind of noble man.

ODE TO THE SUNRISE

As daylight heralds another day,

all the world comes out to play,

now yesterday has gone away,

And tomorrow becomes the hope of today.

And so I wait in anticipation,

to exercise my imagination,

creating this unusual communication,

this ode to the sunrise materialization.

I sit, I watch, I realize,

today is here before my eyes,

and the words can never visualize,

here is my ode to the sunrise.

RAGING TIGER

Raging tiger, this spirit mine

The deer, the fabric of my mind

The eagle here, within my heart

All these creatures is where I start.

The cheetah lending me his speed

The love of God is all I need.

Like the wind caresses the gentle reed

Nature has prepared this seed.

Now I must grow to meet the Son

And hope to make my living fun

I owe it all to the loving One,

The One who made all these creatures one.

MY LITTLE BELL

Ring, little bell, inside my ear,

you bring to me the greatest cheer,

I heard you once the night before,

and made me want to hear it more.

I found that bell some time ago

and now it rings inside me more.

My heart in answer flings wide it's doors,

to hear that sound deep in its core.

Sing, little bell, of noble birth.

While you bring your words to worth.

You say I love you everyday.

'Tis true, I love you, all the way.

INSPIRED

Celebrate a brighter day,

'Cause this is the reason why we pray,

Your heart will sing a brand new song,

As long as you take love along.

To lose the one you hold dear,

Will only justify your fear,

Turn the heavens inside out.

'Cause there's a silver lining, never doubt.

Be with the brighter side of thee,

And this alone will set you free,

Free to fly on the wings of love,

Be free and find the one above.

Freedom's heart inspires true love,

As the wind supports the soaring dove,

Look for things to be alright,

And get down on your knees tonight.

Love, oh love, where can it be?

Take a look inside of me.

Inside of me there is a spark

I put it there, to light your heart.

I LOVE JESUS AND I LOVE MYSELF FOR IT

A finer love shall never be

then the love I found inside of me

strong emotions from inside me sent

to say I love you. Heaven bent.

A force that inspires the heart to long.

Enthusiastically willing thoughts prolong.

This human need for someone warm,

in so doing, I found inward satisfaction,

that is naught but love of myself in action.

For that which flows from the force.

Is a part of it's source.

You see, love comes from love.

I'm sure you know it.

Yes, I love Jesus and I love myself for it.

GOOD MORNING, WORLD

Opening my eyes to see the sun,
Knowing today will bring on the fun.
Life is love's meal to feast upon,
For love is the wake-up call for everyone.

I know the joy of being in the world,
And I feel the love that truth unfurls.
Like a new-born baby, a precious pearl.
I face each day with a positive curl.

Wrapping myself in the unknown hand,
'Cause GOD still lets me walk this land.
Of life's ever-changing plan,
I meet each moment like a fan.

Good morning world is what I say,
As I open my eyes to meet the day.
Oh beautiful life, to you I convey,
All the love I find on my way.

WORDS

Words express our feelings
Ecstatic joy and delight
But some aren't so appealing
When you sit down to write.

So eyes roll up to the ceiling
Looking to see the light
And find their heart and soul concealing
Their wisdom with the right.

Right to know with whom you are dealing
Writing words so appealing
Love, hate and words so thrilling
When words are used to express a feeling.

REALITY

Life is but a fantasy,
And only consist, of what we see,
What we feel, what we smell,
What we hear, and what we tell.
Limits placed, on an unlimited mind,

Is what we know today, as time.
Is that really sunshine, upon your face?
Or did you really see, those stars in space?
Do you really hear, the sounds of the world,
Or is this too, an internal referral?
Life is a reflection, of our inner self,
From which we receive, our health and wealth.
So we're challenged, to solve the riddle.
On which side of the mirror, do we diddle?
From whence come the thoughts
that touch our hearts?
Springing forth, from perceived darkness,
Yet from a light, that out shines many suns.
The light within, that gives us thought,
Is the very one, that lights our hearts.
Then when this fantasy doth end,
You'll probably want to play again.
So fantasize for all you're worth,
For you hold the keys, to life on earth!

LAZY

I don't want to write no more.

Will someone kindly close the door?

But will I let my life become a bore?

As I get lazy, more and more.

'Tis a story, sad, but true,

But it simply means I'm fooling you.

You see, these words you are reading here,

They do not justify that fear.

So if you follow right along,

This poem will soon become a song,

But please don't sing or make a noise,

Just put this down and get your toys.

And now I'm only three years old.

Outside my window it sure is cold.

Then in the snow I cut my hand,

But laziness is where this began.

FRUSTRATION

Yes! You're right, I see the light,
But somehow it's all wrong,
For looking at the truth you sight,
Leaves no shelter from the storm.

I should not be the way I am,
But when I try to change my shame,
You become disdain.
You say you don't believe
I really want to change,
and that I am insane.

Which leaves not room for anything,
Except more mental pain.

FORGIVEN

I never made a mistake,
God's grace has seen me through.
I never made a mistake,
I prayed the whole way through.

I never made a mistake,
Though I may have been dumb as a brick.
I thank God for putting in the fix,
Not I, but Jesus in the mix.

I never made a mistake,
Yet my knees so often quake.
I know I was a sinner,
But my sins, my Christ did take.

I never made a mistake,
That really took me down.
I raised my sinful eyes to Christ,
And peace and love I found.

I LOVED YOU TO BEGIN

MAN:

Let me come and understand,

what exactly is your plan.

There's no other power in the land,

Then what shall I find,

at your command.

Power raging to be free,

Loving kindness, you for me,

An understanding made to be,

A gentle loving part of thee.

GOD:

Loose the power of your loving heart.

Let not your world just fall apart.

Be free and happy as a lark,

You know I loved you from the start.

What you are is around the bend.

That of you which you lend,

That part of you I call my friend.

You see I loved you to begin!

TIME AND SPACE IS OUR POVERTY

The winds of time
Blows deep in the minds of men,
But do they really understand?

Beneath or above, space does play a game,
for space escapes as man remains.
Far in the conscious part of thee
Time and space will surely flee.
Your senses tell of life's true shade,
Then in our dreams this reality does fade.

Where then is truth of time and space?
Space is mind, they do relate,
As five senses do corroborate.
And too, the inter-mind we all know well,
Controls all the body,
Senses as well.
Yes controlled by same, that's where it fell.
Space that is.
But then can such madness be?
Just consider life and reality
comes from the ego we cannot see.
But this will not alter the truth.
Time and space is our poverty.

THE CHALLENGE

A summer morning, thinking of June

the heat of mid-day is coming soon

little by little this moment changed,

now all the windows are wet with rain.

I search for the moment ,

and look for the day,

when sunshine of that morning

is here to stay.

I but the dreamer, with faith I convey,

what time have I, for this follyful play?

Looking to this morning, with hope on my chest,

me, myself and I will do our best,

to learn to grow and pass this test

if you can do better, then be my guest.

THE GREEDY BIRD

People, people, have you heard,
money's going to make your life absurd.
Those that have it, greed for more,
then when they do, their life's a bore.

Some greed for diamonds to the core,
while the greenback dollar becomes a whore.
Nobody knows and nobody cares,
That when they die, they can't take it there.

Deep in the ground, six feet, I know,
and now that house belongs to Joe.
Wild little greedy bird, with men you Play.
Then leaves them all alone,
when death comes to play

THOUGHT AND MIND

I've written all I have to write.

Seems I should call it a night.

But still the words I here resight,

Show thoughts are as endless as the light.

A light will shine within the mind,

and in each corner, a thought you'll find.

So as I grope to find a line,

the words come forth to me in time.

BEACON: PART II

"THE LOVE BEACON"

LOVING DELIGHT

Passion rises in the night
arms caress and hold you tight.
Feeling that the time is right
To bring our loving to the light.

Moving slowly to touch your thighs,
Watching starlight in your eyes
No time to stop and wonder why,
Love makes thinking pass us by.

Moving in, I touch your being.
Moving out, my heart is seeing,
sight found in the sense of touch,
and feeling a love, I need so much.

Suddenly senses zoom out of sight
flying away like a soaring kite.
Compulsion's arms hold on tight.
Love has struck, in the midst of delight.

SICK

Looking to the light of day

Sickness stands to block my way.

Body falls to this mental play,

But with insight, this cannot stay.

What did I do to deserve this pain?

Maybe my mind has something to gain.

But my body would like to make it plain.

Don't let this dumbness happen again.

DESIRE, THE KEY TO LOVE

One day I met a mystery,
that had no door, only a key.
So aimlessly my thoughts elate,
to find the passage to that gate.

Patience, my friend, that key did say,
Rush in now and you'll lose your way.
Step by step is the way to go,
And I will lead you to your goal.

In search of love, you reached for me,
So I hope she lets you, come and see,
And if she leads you to her door,
Stop your search and look no more

DESIRE

Raindrops fell on my lips
to seal my mouth lest I slip.
You see, these thoughts of strong desire
would only serve to light a fire.

A fire burning deep inside
covered only by my pride.
Feelings raging to be free,
A struggle deep inside of me.

Tell her, one says, within a glance,
Be prudent, young man, and hold your stance.
You see, we must give peace a chance.
'Cause love is empty without romance.

LOVE MADE ME IN LOVE

Fluid movement ever here,
loving actions ever clear,
loving intent destroying fear,
so love's emotions gather near.

Safe within the arms of love,
feelings seem so far above,
this struggle push and shove,
when cultivating growing love.

But beneath this raging fire,
Two hearts find love their one desire,
Then take hold of life and call fate a liar,
For sake of love, two hearts conspire.

THOUGHTS OF YOUR WORDS

How do I answer your fears,
when mine have followed me through the years?
Bringing my life sometimes to tears
but regaining my faith, as wisdom nears.

You see a fear comes in the night
of your mind's search for the light.
So remember darling, that when you're right
fear loses power in your sight.

So do not fear or have a doubt,
and you'll see what love's about.
Then stop and let your feelings shout,
to live without love is definitely out.

THE TOUCH

Around the world and back again.
Strange adventures and many friends,
Scenes that cause my heart to grin,
memories of what life has been.

These memories fill my heart with joy.
The joy of one time being a boy.
The joy of sailing ships ahoy.
And life as an international envoy.

Oh what a life. The joy is such,
That mind has grown, I need no crutch.
But this charmed life, doesn't seem so much,
When I have to compare it to your touch.

LOVE SPEAK

Sharing just my point of view.

Taking time to talk with you.

Hope my point finds it's way through.

Don't let it get lost or misconstrued

I love you darling, is easy to say,

But what of the love I must display?

Love consist of thoughs at play.

They're all the love found in a day.

UNDERSTANDING LOVE

Finding what you're all about,
Leaves my mind with little doubt,
That you need time to weed things out,
Or find anxiety beginning to sprout.

Anxiety will wound the heart,
and kill the love that you impart.
I look to find a way to start,
That understanding and loving spark.

Then understanding will make a way,
For how you justify your day.
But this is what I struggle to say,
I love you darling, so run and play.

GOOD NIGHT MY LOVE

Think of love so tender

And nights of close retreat.

That everlasting story,

Of love that's incomplete.

The morning is the foreground,

Where all things must be met.

'Cause this light tells the story,

Of how your life is kept.

While the moon was shining,

The love that you both kept,

Was only physically binding,

And left you while you slept.

THE LOVE WE SHOW

Mind and heart forever clear,
fire of love so close, so near.
Yet one heart may truly fear
when restrictive love is nurtured here.

Free to love, and free to live.
With freedom's heart, we freely give.
Commitments come from a positive,
when love decides the heart will give.

With true love, two hearts will grow,
true to each other, and start to flow
Because of the harmony they come to know,
and the love for each other, that they show.

THE MORNING OF THE NIGHT

I wrote these words by candlelight,

In the morning of the night.

What better time to say I will,

Or think and say I might.

I might decide to come to you,

And tell you that we are through,

But then the time just isn't right,

'Cause it's the morning of the night.

Go east, go west, go north, go south,

Go anywhere you please.

You'll find that love is waiting there,

To knock you to your knees.

So I wait for morning light,

To tell you, you were right.

Love has gone and taken flight,

So blame the morning of the night.

POETRY LOVE

Poetic times and poetic minds,

Help to write, this poetic ryhme.

They reach across the world of time,

To say I wish that you were mine.

The sparkle of a mountain brook,

Helps to identify your look.

And all the love it must have took,

To catch my heart, on your loving hook.

Now maybe it's a waste, I'll find,

This need I have, to change your mind.

But try I must, tho groping blind,

because my heart is on the line.

LOVE'S RESPECT

What person's feelings will I not respect?

When in my soul, I will regret.

What will I do to ease the pain?

When this I know he's God within.

See me perpetrate this wrong,

As if my soul will go along.

Help me, Lord, and teach me right,

And I'll love my brother,

With all my might.

I WANT YOUR LOVE

Wondering how to speak my intent.

Thinking of words I might present.

Hope those words will make you content.

Hoping you will give your consent.

Consent to love, and consent to hold,

I bravely ask you, cause my love is bold.

With affections growing, yet untold,

Please return my love, before we grow old.

WAR, WHAT APATHY

War is the ego trip of a few,
That destroys many, and gains nothing.
More and more the pain and suffering
Experienced by the innocent, in these conflicts,
Cannot, and does not, justify the people
Blindly following their leaders into war.
For their leaders own hunt for glory.
No one can rightfully justify the act of war.
For it denotes the lowest form of uncivilized behavior.
"Thou Shall Not Kill," and war can never justify that.
The world is for all mankind, and no man,
And no leader, and no government has a God-Given right,
To send any man to his death.
The Planet Earth can no longer let this
God-Forsaken desolation, of it's natural beauty,
The people, land, animals, and seas be continued.
She's calling together her flock, to return the peace
She gave in love, and for each of us, to know,
We are one of the same mother, Mother Earth!

We
Are
Responsible

THE BEACON

Life Sometimes takes us to task.

So we seek our knowledge from the past,

Only to learn that life is an ever changing path

That rolls us in and out of the shadows.

Like a captain of your ship a sail,

Without a Beacon, you'll surely fail

To find your way upon the seas of life,

And run a ground in tears and strife.

That's why the Beacon came to be,

To shine its light on you and me,

And help guide us safely to shore,

To be lost in life's seas no more.

by Emerson Custis